Cheerleading

Cheer Squad

Building Spirit and Getting Along

by Jen Jones

Capstone press

Mankato, Minnesota

Snap Books are published by Capstone Press,
151 Good Counsel Drive, P.O. Box 669, Mankato, Minnesota 56002
www.capstonepress.com

Library of Congress Cataloging-in-Publication Data
Jones, Jen, 1976-
   Cheer squad: building spirit and getting along / by Jen Jones.
      p. cm. — (Snap books cheerleading)
   Includes index.
   ISBN 0-7368-4363-9 (hardcover)
   1. Cheerleading — Juvenile literature. I. Title. II. Series.
   LB3635.J65 2006
   791.6'4 — dc22   2005007269

Summary: A guide for children and pre-teens on team work and
sportsmanship in cheerleading.

Editor: Deb Berry/Bill SMITH STUDIO
Illustrators: Lisa Parett; Roxanne Daner, Marina Terletsky and Brock Waldron/Bill SMITH STUDIO
Designers: Marina Terletsky, and Brock Waldron/Bill SMITH STUDIO
Photo Researcher: Iris Wong/Bill SMITH STUDIO

Photo Credits: Cover and all interior photos by Tim Jackson Photography
except p 4-7, Getty Images and p 32, Britton Lenahan. Back Cover, Getty Images.

1 2 3 4 5 6 10 09 08 07 06 05

Table of Contents

The Power of Teamwork

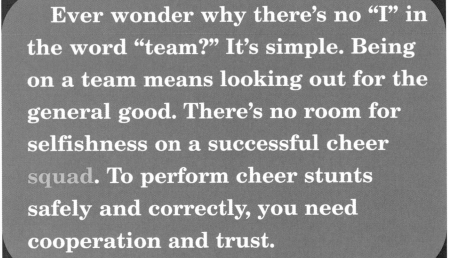

Ever wonder why there's no "I" in the word "team?" It's simple. Being on a team means looking out for the general good. There's no room for selfishness on a successful cheer squad. To perform cheer stunts safely and correctly, you need cooperation and trust.

Becoming closer as a team has to be a group effort. Everyone can work together to learn how to solve problems, talk to each other, and become better leaders. In this book, we'll provide team-building exercises that really work. We'll also give you great ideas for getting to know each other and planning special get-togethers.

Large groups of girls won't always get along all the time. But, when problems do come up, it's important to talk about them and work them out. Respect and understanding are values that everyone on your team should work on building. With these things, your team will go far in **competition** *and* friendship.

" Everyone can work together. "

New Year, New Team

New cheerleaders come through the door every year. Whether you're a returning team member or the new kid on the block, it's always in your own best interest to think of the *squad's* best interest.

To make all of you closer as a team, write up an agreement that lists the squad's goals and rules. It should include a statement that you will each put your own problems aside for the good of the team. Every cheerleader should sign the agreement and get a copy.

Anytime you feel angry, sad, or unsure of yourself, read the agreement to remind yourself of your team's promise to each other.

Since cheerleading is year-round, teammates spend an unusual amount of time together. Wouldn't it be more fun if you considered your team members buddies as well? Check out the games on the next few pages for tips on firing up friendship.

7

Get-To-Know-You Games

You may know who can jump the highest or flip the fastest on your team. But do you know your teammates on a closer level? These fun games will help you get to know each other better and make you become better friends.

Liar, Liar Be careful your nose doesn't grow when playing this naughty game! One by one, each cheerleader must say two true things and one false thing about herself. Everyone else tries to figure out which statement is not true.

Twenty Questions In this game, each cheerleader pairs up with another girl she doesn't know very well. She then asks her 20 questions about herself. When you're all done, everyone tells the group what she learned about her new friend.

Tangled Web All you need for this game is a ball of yarn and lots of good thoughts. One person wraps the end of the yarn around her wrist. She then throws the ball to someone else and tells everyone something she admires about that person. Keep going until everyone has held the ball. At the end, you'll have weaved a web and lots of warm fuzzies!

Guess Who? Get ready for one crazy guessing game! Every girl makes a name tag with her own name on it. All the names are then mixed up in a big bowl or bag. Each girls then pulls out a name tag and puts it on another girl's back. (Make sure it's *not* the girl whose name is on the tag.) Then, each cheerleader walks around the room asking the others questions to figure out whose name is on her back. She can ask things like, "Do I have brown hair?" for clues about whose name is on her back.

C
H
E
E
R
S
Q
U
A
D

M&M Tell-All Pass a bag of M&Ms around a circle and ask each girl to take three. Make each M&M color stand for something that you have to tell the others about yourself. For example, green might be "My Most Embarrassing Moment." Yellow can stand for "My Secret Crush." Every girl then "tells all" based on which color M&Ms she picked. This is one game that's fun *and* yummy!

Take a Seat One of you yells out orders like, "Sit down if you're the oldest child," or "Sit down if you love peanut butter." After each "Sit Down" command, see who's left standing. Then start over with everyone standing back up again, and yell out new "Sit Down" commands.

Building Bonds

Cheerleading is a blast, but its demands on your body can lead to burnout if you're not careful. With all the games, practices, and competitions, it may seem impossible to make time for mischief. But it's still important for your squad to do fun things together all through the season. So get the party started with these great get-together ideas.

Beauty Parlor Party Set up stations like they have in beauty parlors. Make one station for painting your nails, another for doing your hair, and one more for putting on make-up. You'll feel more relaxed *and* more beautiful by the end of the party.

Movie Marathon Snuggle into your pajamas for a night of classic cheer and dance movies. Some perfect picks are *Bring It On!* and *Center Stage*.

Spread the Cheer Go to a game for a sport that your squad doesn't normally cheer for, and make some noise in the stands. The team will be tickled, and you'll have a blast showing your support for them.

Cheer-O-Ling During the holidays, put a twist on the traditional caroling. Entertain your neighbors with holiday songs-turned-cheers. (Make sure to bring a grown-up with you for safety reasons.)

Get the party started!

Have a Little Faith in Me

To be really comfortable in stunting and cheering, you have to trust one another. Trust isn't easily earned, so team-building is important. These exercises will help you bond as a group and learn to trust each other.

Elbow Grease Pair up, standing back-to-back with locked elbows. (One half of each pair holds a pom.) Race to a chosen point and transfer the pom to the other person without unlocking elbows. After the pom pass, the first pair to race back to the other end wins.

Count-by-Numbers Each cheerleader is given a different number. Without speaking or holding up fingers, you all have to use some kind of wacky "sign language" or body movements to let the others know your number. Then everyone must line up in numbered order. This game makes for some very funny moments!

Caterpillar Challenge Each team forms a single-file line, then everyone bends down to grab the ankles of the girl in front of her. The goal is to make it to the finish line first without losing hold. If a "caterpillar" comes apart, that team must start all over again.

"Learn to trust each other."

Ready to set foot onstage? Comedy troupes use exercises like these to feel more comfortable performing together. Since most cheerleaders have great senses of humor, these games should be a breeze.

"Should've Said!" Two cheerleaders perform at a time, making up lines on the spot to scenes like "Birthday Party Chaos." If, at any time during the scene, someone yells, "Should've Said!" the person onstage must change her last line to mean the exact opposite. For instance, "This birthday cake is delicious!" might become "I've tasted better cement cakes!" The "Should've Said" takes the scene in a whole new direction and tests how quickly you can think on your feet.

Bag Ladies Split up into groups of three to five. Each group receives a bag filled with objects from around the house, such as a bar of soap, a fork, and a notebook. Each team then makes up a funny little play using all of the props in the bag and performs for the group.

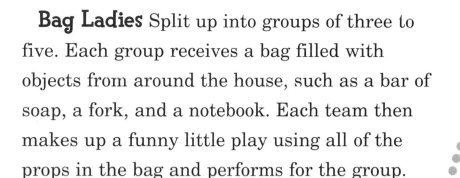

Games like these will put your squad more at ease around each other!

Time to Lead

Cheerleaders don't just lead yells. Most cheerleaders are born leaders and have natural leadership skills. With so many leaders in one group, it's possible that *everyone* might want to take charge. It's important to keep everyone's attention on what's best for the squad as a whole. So having a solid leadership plan *within* the squad is a must.

Taking a leadership role helps squad members feel more like part of the team. Besides captain, there are lots of roles that cheerleaders can fill to make a difference.

The **Messenger Chair** gets the word out about practice plans and schedule changes. She also keeps friends and fans posted on squad news and events.

The **Fund-raising Chair** is all about making money. As the point person for **fund-raising** efforts, she is also in charge of the squad's cash supply (with help from the coach).

The **Uniform Chair** works closely with the coach to select, order, and pass out uniforms and equipment. She should also be aware of the latest fashions in cheerleading.

Selecting a Captain

When choosing a captain, remember to be fair. Don't make a choice based solely on how much you like someone. The right person for captain should have the following qualities:

▶ Friendly yet firm
▶ Keeps things in order
▶ Comes up with great ideas
▶ Fair
▶ Intelligent

A captain's duties include:

▶ Leading practices and cheers
▶ Making up dance numbers
▶ Dealing with team concerns
▶ Working with the coach
▶ Representing the squad as a leader

Team Captain is an enormous responsibility. Only those ready and willing to take it on should do so. Cheerleaders can **nominate** themselves or accept a nomination from someone else. After nominations are made, decide which method of **election** to use.

* Taking team nominations into account, the coach makes the final decision.

* The team casts their votes with the highest vote-getter named captain.

Captain selection puts squad members against each other, so people's feeling may get hurt. Try to respect the team's and coach's decision and move forward with a good feeling about it.

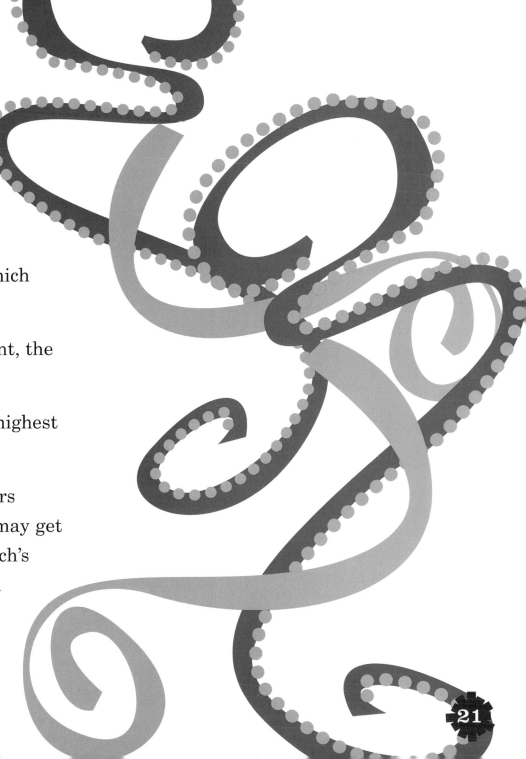

Name Game and Human Knot

Name Game

If you're going to be standing on someone's shoulders, it's important that you at least know her name. This game is a fun way for squads who are bringing together old and new members to get to know each other.

Choose a word that describes you. Make sure that the first letter of that word is the same as the first letter of your name, like "Silly Sally." Each person shouts out her chosen name. Pay close attention, because everyone has to repeat *all* of the names.

Human Knot

Your big mission is to untangle the human knot! Stand in a circle and hold hands with two different people not directly next to you. After hands are locked, everyone must work together to get untangled, *without* letting go of hands. To solve the puzzle, step over, under, and around each other.

If done correctly, the team should end up in one of the following positions.

* In a figure eight

* In a circle within a circle

* In one large circle with people facing in either direction

Cheer Chain and Hallway Hunt

Cheer Chain

The cheer chain is a test of athletic skill, teamwork, and patience. You'll need all these skills in the wide world of cheerleading. Pair up with another person of about the same height. Go back-to-back and interlock your elbows.

Each pair of girls must sit down as a unit, straighten legs in front of them, and stand back up. (Easier said than done!) Once successfully done in pairs, try it in groups of four, eight, or twelve until the whole squad is locked together. If your entire squad completes the challenge, you can consider yourselves as one!

Hallway Hunt

Uncover hidden treasures in this unforgettable exercise. Form three groups. One group decides what things will be "hunted," and the other two teams have a contest to find those things. Give each team a camera and a list of the things they have to try to find. Challenges could include, "Find a yearbook from 1981" or "Take a picture with the coach in the locker room." The first team to find everything on the list is the winner.

"Most" Awards and Turn Over a New Leaf

"Most" Awards

"Most" Awards recognize team members for their special talents. At the end of the season, each girl writes down "Most" Awards on sheets of paper, such as "Most Supported" or "Most Likely to Hit Her Stunts Every Time." After you're finished, put the sheets in bags for each girl and pass the bags out to give encouragement.

Turn Over a New Leaf

For this game, all you need is a tablecloth and great ideas. The goal is to turn the cloth over without touching the surrounding ground. Did we mention that all members must be on top of the cloth at all times? Put your heads together and call on your problem-solving ability to complete the task. (Here's a hint. Holding each other and stunting are allowed.) While you play, think about which areas of the team need improvement and make a promise to "turn over a new leaf."

"Give encouragement!"

Pom Pals and B-I-N-G-O

Pom Pals

Joining a squad can be a bit scary. That's where Pom Pals come in. Have your coach decide which older members will become Pom Pals to which newer members at the beginning of the year. (But keep the Pom Pals' names secret from the younger girls.) For several weeks, the younger cheerleaders must try to guess who their Pom Pals are. Small gifts and hints can be given during this time. Finally, a party is held where everyone finds out who her Pom Pal is. After the secret is out, Pom Pals act as a shoulder to cry on and a friend to call on.

B-I-N-G-O

Hit the team-building jackpot! Each cheerleader should tell the coach something that sets her apart from the others. From that, the coach makes a Bingo card with questions like "Which cheerleader is a triplet?" or "Which cheerleader loves to rock-climb?" Cheerleaders must talk to each other to find out the right answers. Collect signatures in the question boxes. For instance, the rock-climbing whiz signs the "Rock Climbing" box. The first player to get B-I-N-G-O wins.

GLOSSARY

bond (BOND) the feeling of closeness that the members of a team have for each other

burnout (BURN-out) a feeling of being overly tired, worn out, and unable to continue with your duties

competition (kom-puh-TISH-uhn) competing against another team or person

election (i-LEK-shuhn) choosing who will be your leader by placing votes

fund-raiser (FUND RAY-zur) an event put on to raise money for a cause

leadership (LEED-ur-ship) the ability to act as a leader of a team

nominate (NOM-uh-nate) to suggest a person to be put in a leadership role

squad (SKWAHD) a team of cheerleaders

FAST FACTS

* Like cheerleading squads, many companies and sports teams also use team-building activities to raise spirits among workers and team members.

* Cheerleaders are even more athletic than you thought. Sixty-two percent of them are involved in a second sport.

* There are many physical activities and sports that cheerleaders can do together as team-builders. Rock-climbing, paintball, and adventure sports are all great for bringing you closer together as a team.

* The teamwork skills you learn as part of a cheer squad will be useful in many other areas of your life!

READ MORE

Jones, Alanna. *Team-Building Activities for Every Group*. Richland, WA: Rec Room Publishing, 1999.

McElroy, James T. *We've Got Spirit: The Life and Times of America's Greatest Cheerleading Team*. New York: Berkley Publishing Group, 2000.

Newstrom, John W. and Edward E. Scannell. *The Big Book of Team-Building Games: Trust-Building Activities, Team Spirit Exercises, and Other Fun Things to Do*. New York: McGraw-Hill, 1997.

Wilson, Leslie. *The Ultimate Guide to Cheerleading*. New York: Three Rivers Press, 2003.

INTERNET SITES

FactHound offers a safe, fun way to find Internet sites related to this book. All of the sites on FactHound have been researched by our staff.

Here's how

1. Visit *www.facthound.com*

2. Type in this special code **0736843639** for age-appropriate sites. Or enter a search word related to this book for a more general search.

3. Click on the **Fetch It** button. FactHound will fetch the best sites for you!

ABOUT THE AUTHOR

While growing up in Ohio, Jen Jones spent seven years as a cheerleader for her grade-school and high-school squads. Following high school, she coached several cheer squads to team victory. For two years, she also cheered and created dance numbers for the Chicago Lawmen semi-professional football dance team.

Jen gets her love of cheerleading honestly, because her mother, sister, and cousins are also heavily involved in the sport. As well as teaching occasional dance and cheerleading workshops, Jen now works in sunny Los Angeles as a freelance writer for publications like *American Cheerleader* and *Dance Spirit*.

Index